DON'T LET

The Tail

BRING YOU DOWN

Barbara Mitchell
BM Production

All Scripture quotations in this book are from The Authorized (King James) Version. Rights in the Authorized Version in the United Kingdom are vested in the Crown. Reproduced by permission of the Crown's patentee, Cambridge University Press.

Copyright © 2006 by Barbara Rogers Mitchell All rights reserved

This book is dedicated to
Uncle Sam Rogers

Table of Contents

INTRODUCTION	1
CHAPTER 1	5
CHAPTER 2	13
CHAPTER 3	17
CHAPTER 4	27
CHAPTER 5	35
CHAPTER 6	43
CHAPTER 7	47
CHAPTER 8	53
CHAPTER 9	61
CHAPTER 10	71
CHAPTER 11	83
CHAPTER 12	93
Acknowledgments	97
About The Author	99

INTRODUCTION

I grew up in a church, yet I had a common hidden problem that is well known in our churches today. I had a sex addiction, one that controlled and told me what to do and who to do it with. It always dominated my thoughts and emotions. I knew I loved God and had a call on my life. I knew the spirit of God was fighting with the evil spirit that possessed me. No matter how much I tried not to give in to sex, my flesh would always give in to the demon. I wanted to be closer to God, but I just didn't know how to stop fornicating.

I had all the teaching and wonderful examples on living righteous before the Lord. I cannot tell a lie. My parents were among the best role models in the world. These were people who feared the Lord. They were not hypocrites, as some would say. I've never seen my father or mother living an ungodly lifestyle. I choose to go my own way. Nobody's fault but mine.

I was caught up in sin, and I couldn't stop committing fornication. You might be saying to yourself "just stop sinning," right? That's easier said than done. It's not that easy. The devil doesn't play fair! I wanted to stop but could not quit. I never truly knew who was responsible for the lust. Often, I blamed myself, because it had not been revealed who was in control. Yes, I thought it was Satan working alone, but I found out he was not working alone.

For we wrestle not against flesh and blood, but against principalities, against powers, against the rulers of the darkness of this world, against spiritual wickedness in high places. (Ephesians 6:12)

I didn't know at the time I was fighting a spirit. It's her, the woman in Rev 17 that sits on the back of the beast. She is very much alive and very powerful.

She doesn't receive the credit that's due to her. People often blame it on the devil, but he is not alone. Not only does he have a third of the angels now, who are called demons, he has the mother of harlots sitting on his back, helping him conquer and devour.

I worked for her for many years, helping her bring down saved men and confusing the minds of unsaved men concerning church women. I was under the influence of her spell. I had to make the choice to leave her for our Lord and Savior, Jesus Christ. In this book I will show you how the devil and the mother of harlots work together in harmony, hand and hand to destroy preachers, deacons, evangelists, prophets, politicians , artists and more. Rev 17 says this woman who rides on the back of the dragon has the blood of the saints in her. The world needs to know what we are up against. In this book, I will reveal the truth about the devil and the woman who rides on his back.

God's mercy is new every morning, because there are new demons that are more powerful than the demon who attacked you on yesterday. The devil never gives up! Man should always pray and not faint (Luke 18:1).

I pray this book will open your eyes, just as God opened my eyes, so you can be aware of the schemes of the mother of harlots and the devil. Satan is not playing fair. You cannot possibly fight on your own. You need God to be on your side. The Bible says, "My people are destroyed for lack of knowledge." (Hosea 4:6). I pray this book will enlighten your spirit and your mind to keep working for Jesus and not Satan and this mother of harlots.

I encourage you to share this book with your singles' ministries, the young and the old, and also to struggling married couples. It's essential to know the enemy's techniques.

CHAPTER 1

Let's Talk About Sex
Rev 12

I didn't get the revelation of this scripture until I spoke with Uncle Shay. It seems like it was just yesterday when my father called me into his room and asked me to go visit my uncle.

He said, "Bobby, your Uncle Shay is on his death bed, and I know he loves you. And he will listen to what you have to say. Go, see him and make sure he is ready to die. Make sure he has fixed it up with Jesus."

It was such an honor that my father, the late Bishop T.J Rogers, asked me to do this. So I went.

On the way there, I contemplated what I was going to say. When I arrived, my aunt let me in. She walked me into the room where he laid. He was so happy to see his little Bobby Ann.

I waited for the right moment. After a short conversation, I popped the big question.

I said, "Uncle Shay, you know that we all have to leave this world. I would like to know, do you know the Lord?"

Uncle Shay bucked his eyes and sat up on his bed and

yelled, "YES, I KNOW THE LORD. BUT DO YOU KNOW THE DEVIL? DO YOU KNOW ABOUT HIS TAIL? WATCH THAT TAIL! It WILL BRING YOU DOWN. It BROUGHT A THIRD OF THE ANGELS DOWN!"

He laughed and immediately it quickened in my spirit that it's still bringing the saints down. If you want to bring a preacher, musician, singer, songwriter, or mostly any human being down, then immoral sex is the number one leading that's destroying our churches and nations today.

I have been on a mission to enlighten

God's people, concerning the tail. I looked up the word tail in the Dictionary Thesaurus and discovered its many other names such as "rear end, hind part, butt." There were songs out about "Doing the Butt,", "Shake your (a) word," Show me what you are working with, back in the day. They were all referring to the hind part or butt. Of course, the slang word is "booty." (Sorry to all the older saints for saying that word.) This made me wonder why the angels would leave the heavenly host or the very presence of God to be with the devil. How can someone who has experienced God, walked with him, known him for who He is, and yet follow after the tail? Don't play! You know it's happening today. How many homes and churches have been destroyed because preachers, teachers, deacons and even presidents allowed the tail to bring them down? *immoral sex*

First of all, before I go any farther, let's just get the word out of our mouth. Say it with me. Take a deep breath and now let's just say it SEX, SEX, SEX, SEX, SEX SEX and SEX.

Now that was not so bad. Let's talk about sex. Sexual sins are in our schools, churches, work place and even at home. Sex is a word no one likes to talk about in the church. Immoral sexual sins are the most common sin that exists in our church today. Weather it is in homosexuality or with the opposite sex, our churches are infested with sexual sin such as fornicators and adulterers. No, I'm not saying that sex is a sin. God ordained sex for married couples (men and women).

Sex is a beautiful thing to share together with your spouse. The devil has taken it and used it as a powerful weapon against God's people. Growing up, I knew I had a love for God and a calling over my life. Often, I saw the spirit moving in the church and felt the spirit touched me as well. I knew God's spirit was on the inside fighting with the evil spirit that possessed me. My flesh always gave in to the demons, because at the time, Jesus wasn't Lord over my life.

Paul said it best, in Romans 7:21. When I want to do good, evil is present within me. Now, before you stone me for what I did before I got married and said yes to the call over my life, please ask yourself what God saved you from. Now, rejoice with me because the things I use to do, I don't do anymore! Praise be unto God for saving us from all our sins.

The Bible said and they overcome him (which is Satan) by the blood of the Lamb and by the words of our testimony. Please let me testify.

There were so many in the Bible who had issues with

their flesh. No this problem didn't just suddenly appear on the scene, it has been here for a long time. Yes, these are people in the Bible we teach about who were involved in sexual sins. Not only David and his son Solomon, but there are so many who were chosen by God, who allowed the tail to bring them down. These sins include prostitutes, murders and other immoral sexual sins.

Yes these were God's chosen vessels. A couple of examples include Eli's sons, Hophni and Phinehas. (1Sam 1:3) Samson sleeping in the wrong lap-Delilah. (Judges 16:18) And Judah sleeping with a harlot, who turns out to be his daughter-in-law. (Gen 38:14) This is just to name a few. Not only was it happening then it is happening in your churches schools and yes even in your home.

First, I want to take a look at the sons of Eli, Hophni and Phinehas. 1Samuel 2:22 reads,

"Now Eli was very old, and heard all that his sons did unto all Israel: and how they lay with the women that assembled at the door of the tabernacle of the congregation."

The sons of Eli, the priest, slept with the women who attended the church to worship God. Yes, this is happening today. Most unsaved and saved men and women attend church to find a companion.

Please don't get me wrong. The church is a good place to find the right women or become acquainted with a good man. Because the Bible says, whosoever findeth a wife findeth a good thing. (Proverb 18:22) However, when you use church women to prey and you don't pray for guidance, then you are just like Eli's sons. I must say we also have so many women who prey instead of pray as well. However, I will discuss this later on in the book. There are so many pastors who are not addressing the issues concerning sexual sins in our churches. Eli addressed them, but did nothing about it. *1 Samuel 3:13* explains what happened as a result of Eli's neglect to the situation. They all died and were replaced.

"For I have told him that I will judge his house for ever for the iniquity which he knoweth; because his sons made themselves vile, and he restrained them not."
(1 Samuel 3:13)

Yes, these were God's chosen vessels because they were the priests, but they were still involved in sexual sins. If you are a leader and you do not restrain this from happening in your church, God is going to judge you. Put a stop to it now!

Let's look at Samson. He was the strongest man who lived on earth. No one could beat Samson. The enemy used a women name Delilah to find out where Samson's strength laid. Pillow talk caused him to lose his strength and to be crippled by his enemies.

Now, Judah in the bible, slept with a harlot who turns out to be his daughter-in-law Gen 38:14. Please read this story, because they had the nerve to try to stone his daughter- in –law until she revealed the signet, the bracelet, and the staff he left with her after they had sex. Judah was an example of some praise and worship teams leaders. The church will sit the woman down (caught in the act of sexual sins) but will allow the male musician caught with her to continue to play Sunday after Sunday. Judah slept with a prostitute. Judah means praise. Yes, this is evidence that it's in your blood praise and worship leaders.

There are so many leading worship or being used by God, who normally have high sex drives. This is why sexual sins are running rampant in the church. Nobody wants to tell the truth. It's in the bloodline of Judah. When I see a worshipper who has a heavy anointing upon his or her life, I immediately start praying. Stop right now and begin to pray over our leaders that God may give them strength.

I'm not trying to be messy at all. However, we must address the truth. Now if you really think about after praise and worship is over and everybody has gone home with their mates, (single people), you can be a witness that the struggle is real. Your flesh will act up really bad. The out pouring of the Holy Ghost hit the house, and you praised him until you could not praise God anymore. I promise you, as soon as you come out of that Holy Ghost experience and come back down to earth, that lust demon will hit you hard. You will wonder where it came from.

Let's get real about this take over. It's going to take more than just a cold shower to cool this one off. You must pray now for later. Ask God to help you. The devil knows you are weak, and he and the mother of harlots are now ready to take advantage of you during your weakness. You are wide open because you want that feeling you just had with God. Brothers and sisters, when done right, sex gives you a high. It's a feeling like no other and the devil knows it. The devil is a deceiver. Can't nobody do you like Jesus.

Go back into worship. Don't go out to eat. Get into your secret closet until God gives you the strength you need to resist temptation.

How many leaders are still employing call girls and prostitutes? Believe it or not, there are so many leaders who preach and teach but can't get pass this test. I'm telling you it is happening everywhere. From the usher to the bishops, they are going earlier to conferences or staying late in order to be with their harlots. I'm not saying all are doing it, but get real. It is happening in our churches today. They are drunk with sexual sins.

*Rev 17:2 with whom the kings of the earth have committed fornication and the inhabitants of the earth have been made **drunk** with the wine of her fornication.*

Immoral sex is seen on the news about priests, pastors, teachers and deacons who are raping and are involved in all types of sexual immoralities. They are saving thousands of lives but caught up into the sexual immorality trap.

*For what is a man profited, if he shall **gain the whole world**, and lose his own soul? (Matt 16:26) But he shall say, I tell you, I know you not whence ye are; depart from me, all [ye] workers of iniquity. (Luke 13: 27)*

Not only God's chosen but others are affected by sexual sins. Judge 16:18, Shechem the son of Hamor the Hivite caused the men in his entire family to die because he slept with Dinah the daughter of Leah and Jacob, Gen 34:1. How many people have you heard of getting killed because of sexual sins?

Please don't forget about John who was killed for speaking out against adultery. John preached, "Repent for the kingdom of heaven is at hand." He spoke out specifically against King Herod's adultery, and was killed for speaking the truth (Mark 6:25). Yes in Rev 12, the dragon's tail drew a third of the angels. However, after they were drawn in, now you see them willing to fight and kill, even losing their places in Heaven, all because they were drawn in by the tail.

Wake up!

Don't let the devil cause you to lose what you worked so hard to get or what God gave you. I know people will come out against me for talking against fornication and adultery. But I made up my mind that I will be a mouthpiece for my Lord and Savior Jesus Christ. Perhaps this book will not be popular with many, but if I can only reach the remnant that God wants me to reach, my life will not be in vain.

CHAPTER 2

The Forbidden Fruit

"But of the tree of the knowledge of good and evil, thou shalt not eat of it: for in the day that thou eatest thereof thou shalt surely die." (Gen 2:17)

When Adam ate from the forbidden tree, knowledge was birthed into mankind. The five senses: sight, hearing, taste, smell and touch, are now a part of mankind's life. Now man has the physiological capacities of organisms that enable data by perceptions. The ability to feel! The ability to see, the ability to touch and smell was given to man. What a feeling sex gives you. Oh yes it can be really wonderful. Adam and Eve were naked the entire time, but their eyes became open when they bit off the forbidden fruit. Instead of their eyes being on God or their spouse, now there is room for bestiality and other sexual immoralities.

You can never crave something you never had. However, once you have engaged in sexual activities, you will forever desire that particular feeling. When you first become sexually active, your eyes are opened. It opens a door to your spirit man, a revolving door that allows Satan and the mother of harlots (Rev 17) to enter, unless you allow the Holy Ghost to put a lock on that spiritual door. Until God takes it away or until the day you die, you will desire that thing call SEX. This is why you should remain a virgin until you get married.

When their eyes became open, and they were like gods, they knew each other in another way. He knew. Let's be real. Now I'm not saying sex is wrong. It is a beautiful thing between a woman and a man who are married. However, when they ate the forbidden fruit, their eyes became open to immoral sex. That spirit is still active on the inside, and it's going to take God to control it. Just remember.

Sex is a natural thing. Women and men know exactly what to do. Yes, some know a little more than others. However, when mentioned, you get this sexual sensation. This is why sex sales. I will talk about it later on in this book. My perception of how his started. After you have bit off the forbidden fruit, now you are actually craving. It feels as if you can't live without this person.

It has started. You are craving because you are empty. After taking the forbidden fruit Adam and Eve were now craving for the love they once had for God. This is why they didn't not answer God in the garden because they fail out of love with God. Their eyes were now fixed on other things and were no longer focus on their creator. They were already naked and not a shame. However, when they disobeyed God they begin to crave for something other than God.

Now they are searching for leaves to cover the body.

Are you searching now? Are you searching to satisfy the lust and the cravings on the inside? Are you a shame? Ask God to help you. God wants to heal you and set you free. Listen, God had to kick them out of the garden in Genesis 3:23-24 Therefore the Lord God sent him forth from the Garden of Eden, to till the ground from whence he was taken.

Please note the 23rd verse, And the Lord God said, Behold the man is become as one of us, to know good and evil: and now, lest he put forth his hand, and take also of the tree of life, and eat, and live forever: God knew man would crave for another taste. See you have told yourself, "I'm only going to do it one time, after this I will be ok". Now that one time has turned in to 100 times and you don't care who knows it. You are craving like a drug attic or an alcoholic. Now you need your next fix.

At first you had some dignity about yourself and certain people you didn't have sex with, but now you are a sex attic and you can't get enough. Are you craving for sex? Are you craving in lust and about to give in to this lust demon? If you answered yes, you have been caught up into the web of lust. You are in it and you can't get out of the web of lust.

First you listen to the spirit in your head that told you, you really needed someone or something to help you satisfy this craving. Now you actually believe what's in your head and now you are looking. People or even things that you normally don't give a second look to, you are now looking or searching for that satisfaction. After you find that person or something, you will begin to lust after it.

This is the time you really need to pray because now you are getting ready to do it. You need it and you need it right away. You are craving because you are empty. The word of God said be filled with the spirit Ephesians 5:18. Ask God to fill you up and let it overflow. He did it for me and I know he will do the same for you.

CHAPTER 3

Who's Your Mother

The dragon pulled the angels down with his tail. Don't get all deep with me. You know he is still pulling people down with the tail. His tail draws.

We will go deeper in chapter six concerning the sexual sins of angels. I want to enlighten you on the fact that Satan does not work alone. His partner is the mother of harlots. We read about her earlier in the book of Revelation 17:5.

If you are committing fornication or adultery, she is your mother. If you are having sex and you are not married to the person you are having sex with, she is your spiritual mother, YO momma! I know you don't want anybody to know who she is because she doesn't have a good reputation. If you examine yourself you will realize you don't either. Check yourself! Who's your Mother?

"So he carried me away in the spirit into the wilderness: and I saw a woman sit upon a scarlet colored beast, full of names of blasphemy, having seven heads and ten horns. And the woman was arrayed in purple and scarlet colour, and decked with gold and precious stones and pearls, having a golden cup in her hand full of

abominations and filthiness of her fornication. And upon her forehead was a name written, **MYSTERY, BABYLON THE GREAT, THE MOTHER OF HARLOTS AND ABOMINATIONS OF THE EARTH.** *And there came one of the seven angels which had the seven vials, and talked with me, saying unto me, Come hither; I will shew unto thee the judgment of the great whore that sitteth upon many waters: With whom the kings of the earth have committed fornication, and the inhabitants of the earth have been made drunk with the wine."*
(Revelations 17:1-5)

I'm sorry I didn't give "the mother of harlots" her proper introduction. No, she doesn't receive the credit that's due to her. She is the mother of harlots sitting on Satan's back (the dragon),, helping him conquer and devour all they can. The Bible says the devil or the adversary goes to and fro throughout the earth seeking whom he may devour (2 Peter 5:8). This mother of harlots assists Satan, working hard trying to destroy us. The woman who rides on the back, she seduces you and the devil draws you. Yes, they work together. Who is this woman?

"So he carried me away in the spirit into the wilderness: and I saw a woman sit upon a scarlet colored beast, full of names of blasphemy, having seven heads and ten horns." Revelation 17:3

She is the very root of harlots. Her spirit is in every sexual sin such as fornication and adultery. No I don't hate any particular sin, but the Bible is clear on right and wrong. I have friends who are fornicators now, and I committed fornication before I married (tell the truth and shame the devil). Also, I have friends who committed adultery (some are straight and some are gay). It doesn't matter.

Sin is sin! Repent.

Jesus is soon to return. I love everybody, and I respect their choices. Meaning I do not judge or beat up on anyone, but we should always tell the truth!

Sin is sin!

When I am wrong, I want my friends to be honest with me. Nobody is perfect, but we have to encourage one another to turn from our sinful ways, so we can be ready when Jesus comes back. **Repent for the Kingdom of Heaven is at hand!** The Bible is right and somebody is wrong!

For too long the church has remained silent. It has become a conspiracy that if anyone speaks out against her (the mother of harlot), then she has vowed to destroy them or discredit them. John was beheaded by Herod in Mark 4 14:29 because he spoke against the adulterous spirit. This mother of harlots is proud of her job. She will cause a person to do anything for money and just to feel good. She is the spirit of Lust working heavily, hand and hand with Satan.

She makes lots of money too.

Rev 17:4 And the woman was arrayed in purple and scarlet colour, and decked with gold and precious stones and pearls, having a golden cup in her hands.

She is not BROKE BABY. Take a look at porn stars and prostitution. No they are not broke. They got that money. No problem. Kings, businessmen, preachers, presidents and others make sure they stay in business. Oh yes its real.

Look out. I may be talking about your leader or even YOU. Yes she has some of the saints inside of her. Pay attention to Rev 18:4. Come out of her!

And I saw the woman drunken with the blood of the saints.

Revelation 17:6

The enemy will fight to make sure you do not reach the top until he has some good gossip on you to silence you when necessary. Sin is Sin. If I'm wrong, tell me to repent for the Kingdom of Heaven is at hand. If your family members are wrong, please tell them to **repent.** (Repent for the Kingdom of Heaven is at hand)

Speak out just as the prophet Jeremiah did. Oh, no I'm not perfect. I'm far from perfection. But we must tell each other the truth and make the saints aware of the enemy's tactics. Lest Satan should get an advantage over us. **"For we are not ignorant of his devices."** 2 Corinthians 2:11

Yes, this enemy has been exposed. God will avenge you, servants of the highest God. God will judge the great whore, which did corrupt the earth with her fornication according to Rev 19:2.

"And I heard another voice from Heaven saying Come

out of her, my people, that ye be not partakers of her sins, and that ye receive not of her plagues." (Rev 18:4)

We will discuss more in Chapter five about the exit out of her. If at any time you feel as if you want to get up and leave her now, Jesus has open arms waiting on you.

Do it NOW!

I want you to know demons are real and powerful, but Jesus got up with all power. Temptations are in some singles as well as married people. It doesn't matter if you are a sinner or a saint. It's very hard to fight temptation and stay celibate as a single person. Saints we need the power of the Holy Ghost to keep us from falling. I had to learn the hard way.

It's hard to be married and not as sexually active as you were prior to getting married. If you think it was hard while you are single, then don't get married. The demons will torment you day and night if you have not been totally delivered. This is why there are so many separations and divorces in the world today.

He will cause your spouse to cheat, just to get you to cheat. This demon wants you to go back to your old ways. Ask God to take control of your life. Start today. It's not too late. He can help you remain celibate until he sends you the right spouse.

Tell God to take away the lust. "Take it away Lord." The spirit of Lust is very dangerous. Lust will cause you and your entire family to die as I stated before. It will drive you out your mind. I pointed out the scripture Revelation 17:6. She was drunk with the blood of the saints, and with the blood of the martyrs of Jesus. *"With whom the kings of the earth have committed fornication, and the inhabitant of the earth have been made drunk with the wine of her fornication."* Also, Revelation 17:2 says she is like a vampire who puts her venom in you and causes you to get drunk. This is why she will have you so out of your mind that you don't know which way to go. Lust is no joke. Lust will have you craving like a crack head.

If you think Lust just started in recent times, think again. Look at a great number of leaders you know.

Now, I'm not saying all of them, but some leaders live under the influence of sexual immorality. They are drunk with sexual sins. God has blessed them and given them almost everything, but they are sleeping with everybody. Growing up, I would often hear my mother talk about a great preacher who lost his life because of sexual sins. He was caught cheating with one of his church members.

Don't try to fool me. You know I'm telling the truth. They are having affairs and partaking in sexual immorality. Now this is my personal opinion. I believe some of them truly love the Lord but need deliverance in that area.

How do I know? Before I got married I had the same problem. Loving God but having issues with my flesh.

I will share my story later on in this book. The way to her getting drunk with your blood is simple. It starts out with one sip. Perhaps some of you have gone out for drinks back in the day before you were converted. You buy one drink, then another. Before you know it you have lost count and now you are unable to drive home because you are drunk. The devil will have you sipping by getting that phone number or that eye contact. You know he or she likes you, but you are married or know you are easy like Sunday morning.

Instead of leaving before it makes you fall, you stay to get the feel good, ear full of pleasant words. You have not had this much attention since your honeymoon. Your spouse is not giving you enough time, so he or she is giving you all their time. They just want to be with you, just want to talk.

STOP SIPPING! Yes you are sipping and about to get drunk. Baby release that conversation and GET OUT OF THERE! NO you are not strong enough to handle that Spirit. She will bring a giant to his knees. She will make a strong woman weak.

These spirits will cause you to start sipping until you start fornicating and committing adultery. It happens in the mind first. Looking at the magazines going onto the porn sites, talking on Facebook, Twitter, etc. You know he or she is not good for you. However, you just keep right on sipping. If you keep sipping you will fall into the trap of the devil and this harlot.

I'm not just talking about women, but men as well. **Come out of her.**

If someone is trying to cause you to sin against GOD, RUN, RUN, RUN. Brothers and sisters, I was once an enticer and one thing I know about enticing, is that 80% of men and women fall for the trap.

Run just as Joseph did when Potiphar's wife tempted him, Genesis 39:12 Touch your neighbor and say, "flee. " Run. Run. Run. I will talk more about this later on in the book.

We see it on the news—priests, pastors, teachers, deacons, Christian singers and others exposed concerning sexual sins. No one is exempt from falling into this trap.

Saving thousands of souls, but they are drunk on the fornicating or adultery spirits. Believe me when I say, this is alive and well in our world today. When the fornicating spirit gets you drunk, you are out of it. You remembered at first. You were trying to hide. Now you don't care if someone sees you. Nothing really matters. It doesn't bother you if your wife or husband leaves. You don't care what your family members think or how your children see you.

YOU ARE A DRUNKEN MAN, WOMAN, BOY OR GIRL!

Stop sipping on her lust juice. You know when something doesn't feel right. Don't be foolish. Get your mind back. Ask God to help you, and run for your life. I don't care if he or she is the only one, and it seems as if they are so sweet. They are employed by the devil and the mother of harlots. If they want you to commit sexual sins, they are being used by Satan and this woman.

Listen, I know you are asking, "How are you going to know if you are truly delivered until you have been tried and proven?"

Well, I come to expose this spirit. Do not, and I repeat, do not try to prove anything to anybody. Run for your life. Your life depends on you running.

If you want to live holy and walk the straight and narrow way, you must first pray and ask God for His guidance. The Holy Spirit is not going to tell you to sleep with someone that you are not married to.

While I'm on the subject of marriage, I speak against same sex marriages. God loves everyone, but God hates sin. I believe the Bible concerning same sex marriages. Please repent before it's too late.

Now don't stop reading this book because you don't like what the Bible says about same sex marriages. No hate here, only love for you my sisters and brothers. Perhaps I may go to jail for this, but if Peter, John, Paul and others went to jail for speaking the truth, then so be it. I do not hate anyone. Those who know me, know I love everybody. As I said before the Bible is right and somebody's wrong. The truth sometimes hurts, but it helps.

I speak to homosexuality and lesbianism. "Be set free-- be delivered today" in Jesus name. I speak deliverance over your life today. Come out in the name of Jesus. I know the world tries the cars and other material things out first, "Try before you buy" or you have a 30-day return policy, but we are not like the world. "We are in the world but not of the world." We are not supposed to operate like the world.

Pray and seek God. If God said it, that settles it. Prayer will make it all right. Trust God.

CHAPTER 4

Deal With It

We are people who love to do things that are forbidden. Just think when you were single. You thought sex was the world with your boyfriend or partner, who is now perhaps your spouse. After you married, sex was not the number one priority. Before you married, it seemed as if you needed sex every night and day. Wake up. Now that you are married, you are having the same sex with the same person as before. However, now it's legal with God. Now, six months later, sex is just okay. This is why the interest goes quickly outside the marriage. It's legal with GOD.

The devil is playing God's people like a deck of cards. The devil is redundant in this game of life. He has played the same game over and over again. I was born to expose the devil and this mother of harlots. They are using the power of sex to bring you down. No you are not hot or horny every second and every minute. It is a demonic force trying to overtake you.

I must be honest with you. I married because I felt I could not abstain from having sex.

I prayed this prayer. "Lord, I love you with all my

heart, but I can't stop having sex. Will you please send me a husband that will satisfy all my needs?"

God did just that. I met my husband. He satisfied all my needs. But guess what. The spirit of fornication was still inside of me. It was only suppressed.

Later on in my marriage, he started to stay out. I caught him cheating. Later, his lovers started calling my house. I was devastated, and even after he was caught, he continued to stay out sometimes for two and three days.

My body was in a frenzy. I wanted sex so bad. Yes, I was an evangelist, and yes, I was singing. No, you don't want to hear the truth, but the struggle was real. My body was crying for attention. See if you don't get rid of that spirit when you are single, you will have a tough time getting rid of the fornicating spirit when you are married. When you have been made drunk with fornication, you become addicted to it. It's like being on crack, alcohol and any other abused substance.

I went through detoxification. My body craved sex and affection from someone else.

I'm telling you, during this time I didn't know I was an addict. I thought I recovered after I married my husband. My body was not over it at all. I had to confront it. I cried myself to sleep in the bed all alone, because I knew he was with another woman, and I could do nothing about it.

I wanted to leave. God spoke to me and said, "Why? So you can suppress this demon again."

Yes. That was my intention. Go marry another man, because I could not stay saved and be single. So I thought.

I thought I had to have it every night, until my

husband stopped coming home every night. The nights were lonely—very lonely. One night, I was alone on my sofa. I heard the demons calling me, saying, "Go get you somebody. You look good. You don't have to take this."

Then I heard the Holy Spirit say, "You can either fall in my arms or fall into another man or women's arms."

I chose Jesus that night. I told God to hold me.

I remember holding a pillow so tight and not letting it go.

I told God, "I refuse to go back."

You have to make up your mind to choose God. You are going to hear this throughout this book. The devil is not after your spouse. He may already have your spouse. He wants you. They want you; they are trying to play you like a deck of cards.

Fall into the arms of Jesus. He's waiting on you. This is the time for you to seek Him. Get closer to Him. He wants to take you higher and give you a greater anointing. Read the word of God and just tell God to have His way in your life—help you to stand, help you to hold out. He will do it now.

God spoke to me and told me to deal with it. Get it all out of your system. Cry if you must. Pray or sing—whatever you have to do, do it. When this is over you are going to be clean. Women and men, you cannot go on to another relationship until you get this fornicating demon out of your system.

Don't get me wrong, God will preserve the desire until you get married. Trust me. I know it's hard, but this is for your sake.

DEAL with it. Pray. Fast. Do whatever it takes and deal with it.

Yes, you are going to have to **Deal With It**, before it deals with you. Many single people say, "If I had a husband or wife, I could truly live for you Lord."

If you think living for God is hard being single, then you are in for a big surprise when you get married. As I said before, you are going to face this demon again. In my experience as a wife, I didn't know I had to seek God even more. For you see, that man who I once committed fornication with every night before we got married did not change, but his desire changed. Before we got married, I felt guilty every time I had sex because I knew what I was doing was wrong. It was against what I was taught as a child about the Bible and I knew God was not pleased. When I married him, the guilt was gone. People are attracted to things that they aren't supposed to have. This is why our sex life was so strong because the devil and this woman used me against God. This made God hurt, and the devil loved it. Thank God for the blood of Jesus who has washed us from all our sins. Now, I'm married, and it's legal, so it's not hurting God. It's hurting the devil.

Then, the devil makes your spouse act a fool so you can go out there and get somebody else to sin against God. It's the same old game the devil has been playing for centuries. So he already has you cheating on your spouse. Repent today, and ask God to help you.

Run Run Run!

If the enemy has put the thought of cheating in your mind, don't do it. Don't do the crime if you don't have the time. Every time you commit adultery or fornication you have a setback. I don't care if you're still active in your local or national church. Perhaps, everybody knows your name. You are still mentally set back.

When you least expect it, the enemy is going to bring it up before God. Yes, God will forgive. However, there are consequences for our sins. Consequences such as AIDs, disease and unwanted pregnancies, sometimes even death, after you've been caught. Ask God for deliverance.

Jesus has everything you need. He satisfies.

I know you are in your home, and you are very lonely right now. But I'm telling you this is the time to get to know Him better. Cry out to Jesus and tell Him you are hurting, and you need His assistance.

In our weakness, He is made strong. (2 Corinthians 12:9) Be honest with God. You need to deal with the fact that your nature is high. David and Solomon's nature was high as well. Deal with the fact that you want some, and you want it now. Deal with the fact that you are lonely, and you need to be comforted.

Face the fact that your body is out of control. Deal with those desires you have on the inside. If you have a desire in your heart to cheat, then tell God. He already knows. Tell him to take it away. I'm a witness, He will.

I know the church folks are saying she is carnal, but if the truth be told, we all have our carnal days. This is a spirit, so you must get in the spirit to fight the spirit. No, you cannot fight what you can't see. However, when you get into the spirit, the spirit will show you what the devil and this woman are planning.

I know right now you want vengeance, but as previously referenced, vengeance belongs to the Lord. Yes, your spouse may have been caught red handed, but you got to get into your place and pray. You don't have to be on your knees with your eyes closed. Wherever you are reading this book, just stop and pray. Pray in your heart, and God will hear you. For now, you need to get to know Him better. Tell God this is an opportunity to get closer to Him. This is a chance to fall into His arms. I'm telling you He has his arms wide open, just for you. Just do it now.

Revelation 17:18 "And the woman which thou sawest is the great city, which reigned over the kings of the earth."

In God's eyesight, we as believers are cities with our own light in this dark world. **_Matthew 5:16 Let your light so shine before men, that they may see your good works and glorify the Father in heaven._**

God gave us all a little light and some people continue to let it shine and others allow their lights to go out. This can be seen in Matthew 25:1 concerning the ten virgins who all had lights and went to meet the groom. Five were wise and five were foolish. The wise took extra oil with their lamps and the foolish only took their lamps and what was in them. The Bible says while they were all sleeping, there was a cry saying the bridegroom is coming. The foolish allowed their lights to go out.

Don't be a fool by not taking the extra oil and letting your light go out. God showed me in the spiritual realm just as it is in the flesh. Cities have states and states have capitals. This woman is the head of all spiritual cities who commit fornication and is an abomination in this world. She is the capital of all cities that partake in her lust. She wants you to be a part of it.

The Word of God says in Isaiah 5:14, "Hell hath enlarged herself and opens her mouth without measure." Yes they want you to be a part. For you see in Ephesians 5:5, "But fornication and all uncleanness or covetousness, let it not be once named among you as you become saints. Old things are passed away behold all things have become new.

Remember Jesus said in Matt 5:14, "Ye are the light of the world. A city set on the hill cannot be hid." Jesus did not say we were like a city. He said we were a city. A city that is set on a hill cannot be hid. Yes this means you and me. In Rev 17:18, the woman which thou sawest is the great city, which reigneth over the kings of the earth. This means that her city is the capital city over your city if you are committing fornication or adultery.

Ask God to come into your life and be Lord. He is waiting on you. We have enough Christians who thank God for the power of the cross. However, they are not using the power of the cross. Jesus died that we might have victory over our addictions. Yes, I'm saying sex, sometimes, can be an addiction in our minds and spirit. We need the power of the Holy Ghost to help us.

CHAPTER 5

Don't Be a Fool

The mother of harlots and the devil will make you believe the life you live has nothing to do with your anointing until you hit rock bottom. After you hit rock bottom, then you will realize you have left the presence of God and his anointing. Preachers, teachers, and evangelists, start listening to your preaching cd's if you are involved in a sinful relationship. Then listen to how the devil and this mother of harlots is keeping you from preaching what God wants to say.

In today's society, God is saying the wages of sin is death, but the gift of God is eternal life (Roman 6:23). "Woe unto the pastors that destroy and **scatter** the **sheep of my** pasture," saith the LORD (Jer. 23:1). There are a great number of church leaders who dare not preach about this because they are under the influence. Again, I know I will be under great fire for writing this book, but I have been ordained by God to let the world know about this mother.

She doesn't want the world to see her as she is. She is getting ready to be revealed. Don't share in this woman's punishment because she will receive double according to her works.

Let's look back at Revelations 17:4. She is in her royal state. Purple meaning royalty. She is getting everything she wants by working her body.

As I stated in chapter two, she is not broke. Precious stones and pearls—she wears the finest jewelry and has the best of cars and houses, but her end is soon to come.

I know you can't imagine prostitution going out of business, but according to this scripture, they will eventually end.

I must tell you, many women and men are selling their bodies in so many different ways in the church, on the job and everywhere. Come out of the mother of harlots today, and don't wait. I know right now it seems like you can have everything if you work that body, but all will come to an end. I plead to you to come out of her (the mother of harlots).

And I heard another voice from heaven, saying, **Come out of her**, *my people, that ye be not partakers **of her** sins, and that ye receive not **of her** plagues.*
(Rev 18:4)

God is calling. Answer the call. Say, "Yes Lord."

Change your number. Drive another way. Get out of sight, and get on your knees and pray. Destruction is near!

God spoke with me and shared this scripture concerning the children of Israel when they crossed the Red Sea. The reason he closed the Red Sea, not only to keep the enemy from getting to the children of Israel, but so the children of Israel could not go back to the enemy, which was Egypt. You remember they were complaining saying

Moses brought us out here to die. "You should have left us in Egypt, and at least we had food."

God erased the path to Egypt, erased the way back to the place that bound and enslaved them. Sin is a slave master. I remember going through a lust experience. I wanted to fall. Yes I wanted to cheat. I would text every day and plan to cheat. I heard the voice of the Lord say, "Erase the number." I did. God wants to erase the path, but you must do something. Erase that phone number. Erase that address or email address.

God wants to use you and even past experiences yet erase the path that leads back to your old ways. Day by day the mother of harlots works on your mind and your spirit. After erasing the number I tried to find a way to contact him. I wanted to cheat on my husband because I was tired of him cheating and wanted to get back at him. God convicted me in service that day as the preacher was preaching. I erased it again. I'm not ashamed to share. I struggled but God help me get through it. Remember, Jesus said in Luke 18:1, "Man should always pray and not faint." Again, in John8:3, there was a woman, who was getting ready to be stoned because she was taken in adultery. She was caught in adultery, but what happened to the man who was with her? For you see, this is why Jesus said,

"He that is without sin among you, let him first cast the first stone. And they which heard it, being convicted by their own conscience, went out one by one, beginning at the eldest, even unto the last: and Jesus left alone, and the women standing in the midst." John 8:7, 9

I truly believe some of those men, who had a stone ready to kill the lady caught in the very act of adultery had been with this lady in a sexual way. There was a deacon whom once said to me, "Three things that will destroy a church; that's gossip, money, and women."

This is how most males think about how the church runs. The one thing that deacon left out was men. Men and women will destroy a church faster by sleeping with everybody in the church. I remember ministering to a young lady who was hurt by the church. She became pregnant. After the pastor found out she was pregnant, he asked her to step down from singing in the choir. However he allowed the musician who got her pregnant to continue to play. He was the Pastor's son. So many looked down on her but continued to shout when the musician played that shouting music.

Isn't it funny how the pastor will sit the ladies down when they are committing fornication or adultery, but will continue to let the man keep his position whether he's a choir director, musician, deacon, or assistant pastor? It's so funny how some men believe women are the cause of their fall. They are saying, "She shouldn't have worn that dress," or "she was flirting with me."

Men and women are weak when it comes to Lust. "Finally my brethren, be strong in the Lord and in the power of his might. Put on the whole armor of God, that you might be able to stand against the wiles of the devil." (Ephesians 6:10)

I come to tell you, it doesn't matter if you are a male or

a female.

The mother of harlots is after you. She wants you to become a loyal customer. Proverbs 7:7 says, "She is looking for the simple ones, a man void of understanding." If you keep falling into the same old trap, you are simple and you just don't understand.

PUT ON YOUR ARMOUR. Without it, you are going to lose this war.

There are many people caught up in sexual relationships with someone else's spouse. You would not believe how many people (including church people) who are allowing the mother of harlots to have control over their lives. She has many on the inside of her and she is causing them to commit adultery or fornication.

I'm talking to every leader or pastor who has a church. If you know your members are sleeping with others in your church or out of the will of God, please tell them the truth. Right is just right and wrong is just wrong.

Often the leaders are not saying anything because they are living in the same house with long-time lovers. The old folks call it shacking. As a woman of God, I want to let you know their blood is going to be on your hands. Stand for righteousness, and tell the truth. Even if they do not listen, continue to preach holiness. In the day we live in, people do not care what is exposed because they believe everyone is having illegal sex. They act like it is okay, as long as you do it with the opposite sex. This is how stupid this woman has caused some of the saints to be.

Satan never seeks to have someone who he already possesses. He wants someone who belongs to someone else. We all know we belong to God. Satan is jealous of the relationship you have with God. He has been kicked out of Heaven, and he wants you to renounce your rightful place in Heaven. My brothers and sisters, you can't do whatever feels right to you.

"In those days there was no king in Israel; but every man did that which was right his own eyes." (Judges 17:6) They began to make idol gods. How can something feel so good, yet be so wrong? Wake up! You know he or she is not right for you.

God has given everyone the right to the tree of life (Revelation 22:14), but you have to make a choice. There is a remnant of chosen vessels God has chosen to fulfill His will and to do the work of the Lord. "Many are called, but few are chosen." (Matthew 20:16) And the devil sees you as a target.

Satan desires to sift you as wheat (Luke 22:31). He wants to destroy you. He comes to steal, kill, and destroy (John 10:10). You may be rich or poor, attractive, unattractive, popular or not known at all. The devil wants you dead. He does not care who he uses. He wants you so bad. But thanks be unto God for Jesus praying for us (Luke 22:32). Thank God for Jesus interceding for us before the Father, praying daily on our behalf (Romans 8:34).

Go ahead and open your mouth to take this precious time to give God the glory! Thank your Jesus.

You are worthy to be praise. We love you Lord. It is always in order to give God praise. He can and will deliver you from this harlot and the devil.

He did it for me.

Later in this book I will share with you how I allowed the devil to use me at a young age.

Listen, if you are offended so far, concerning the things I'm sharing with you, perhaps you have a demon inside that doesn't want you to read this book. As a matter of fact, it will be hard to finish because the devil wants you ignorant. The scripture clearly says in Hosea 4:6, "My people perish (are destroyed) for lack of knowledge." Today you can no longer say, "Well I didn't know." I'm exposing the devil and this harlot. "Lest Satan should get an advantage of us; for we are not ignorant of his devices." (2 Corinthians 2:11)

The devil is tricky. He is a deceiver. Perhaps, some of you are turned off because I'm talking about Satan an awful lot. I understand, but the Bible clearly tells us we are in a war. Satan is already defeated, I get it. However, to live a victorious life on this earth, you need to know the strategies of the enemy.

When my sons played football, they would say, "Mom, we need to go watch film."

I asked, "What film?"

They replied, "Film of the opposing team."

Now, you know I wanted to know why, right? They shared with me that their coaches and all their teammates sit down to watch the upcoming opposing team to find out their weaknesses as well as their strengths.

Did you not know the devil has studied you? He knows what makes you happy, sad or even horny. Yes I said it. Now you need to study him and his devices.

He is a thief. What do you think he is trying to steal

from you? Your car, house, money or land? Really? He doesn't need any of that.

When he took Jesus up on a high mountain in Matt 4:11, He showed Jesus all of the kingdoms of this world and their splendor (magnificence). Meaning the beauty the world had to offer. He doesn't need your little house, car or money. He has all of that. He wants your mind. He wants your soul. Watch that tail, study the dragon's tail, my uncle Shae said, "It will bring you down." And he was right.

CHAPTER 6

Angels Falling Because of Sex

This generation is asking a lot of question. I pray that you ask God to open your eyes to this great dragon.

Let's look at the book of Revelation 12. These angels wanted something forbidden by God. In this biblical chapter, it describes the scene before the beginning of time—before the earth was completed and before man was formed.

There was a woman in heaven getting ready to deliver a son. The devil was trying to destroy this child. Perhaps you may have had this verse explained in a different way. However, God gave this revelation to me.

The angels fought and were kicked out of Heaven. Now, when we study Revelation we must refer back to Genesis to understand the final book of the Bible.

Genesis 1:2-3, says God moved upon the darkness and said, "Let there be light." The devil is the prince of darkness, and he was cast down to Earth causing the planet to obtain darkness. Some of the writings in Revelation should have been in Genesis so we understand the devil was in the garden. He was cast out of Heaven in Genesis because of the fight recorded in Revelation.

Before we go further into this treacherous woman, let's look at what happens when you're in darkness. I know you don't want to say angels have desires, but you be the judge.

In Genesis 6:2, the sons of God, which were the angels, saw the daughters of men and found them desirable. And they slept with the women. The children who were born

to this unnatural union were giants and abnormal (Gen 6:4).

It was so bad the Bible says they did whatever they wanted to do and God repented that he made man. But, he took pleasure in Noah's family. (Gen 6:13)

I am saying the angels were brought down not only because of pride, but they were also brought down because of lust, by the tail or sexual desires. Satan somehow drew them and won them over to believe he was right and what he was fighting for was right.

You don't have to believe what I'm saying—go read it again. Think about what makes people leave their home, their beautiful home, for some no good man or woman. They will leave church because you mistreated their lovers who happen to be somebody else's spouse.

It will cause you to fight battles that are not even yours. Lust will cause you to kill someone in order to lay with their spouse (David). David had a man killed all because of lust. It will cause you to date people you don't even want. This is a spirit. What makes a woman leave her four children and run away and not care about what she left behind? Lust is a powerful tool the devil is using on the saints. The saddest part? It seems no one is paying any attention.

Watch the devil's pattern. He uses the same one over and over again. He is redundant. The devil does not have enough sense to think of anything new, because the old strategies always work. He has no new ideals, just the same old ones that keep working on the saints.

When Eve talked with the serpent, he said, "You will not die, and your eyes will become open. You will not be like every other creature on earth (having sex only to breed), but you will desire affection and attention." That is what he meant. You will see what you have and start playing around with it. Ever since that day, men and women have been playing around with sexual sins. This is why Adam and Eve lost their home, talking to the devil.

The devil had killing on his mind in Heaven. Yes, this all took place in Heaven. This is why there will be a new Heaven and a new Earth, because trouble occurred in the old Heaven. Hatred was there. Jealousy was there, and fighting broke out there.

Angels were split up there. Just imagine with me. You are working with your co-workers and a third of the workers go on strike because of confusion. You better believe you will know someone out of that bunch. Some friends perhaps broke up over the tail. I'm telling you, when you follow behind the tail you are blind. Now, you really don't care about your family, friends or your job, when you are under the influence of the tail. You just want what you want at that very moment.

For those who have not experienced the drawing of the

tail, it makes you forget about losing everything. It's called being caught up in the moment. If the angels left their homes and friends, how about you or your spouse or your children. Yes, I'm talking about everyone. If you are drunk on this harlot's wine, please know you will be out of control for sure. You must pray without ceasing.

The devil is after your position. He will cause your spouse to be unfaithful only to distract you from keeping your eyes on God. The devil wants you to go back to what you were doing before you got saved. He wants you to cheat. He already has your spouse, and now, he is after you. If you go back into your sinful nature, it will be worse this time. There will be seven more demons that will come and attach themselves to your spirit (Luke 11:26). I'm telling you women and men of God, I know you want to cheat or perhaps have sex before marriage. Don't do it. You may feel an urge to do it, but please turn your face toward God and say, "Help me."

Perhaps you feel justified, because everybody else is doing it. Your spouse is doing it. Your neighbors are doing it. Even your pastor may be doing it.

The devil will put people around you to cause you to think everybody is out of the will of God concerning sex. But some people are truly sold out to the Lord. You have to make up your mind that this body belongs to the Lord.

Repeat after me "The devil is defeated." Keep saying it until your very soul is convinced that he is defeated. Let the Holy Spirit be Lord over your body. You have the victory in Jesus.

Believe it! Don't fall for that trap. It is the trick of the enemy when you feel you are the only one trying to live for God.

CHAPTER 7

Who Will Be Able to Stand

My mind goes back to 1 Kings 18-19 when Elijah was running from Jezebel, and he felt he was the only one living right. God responded to him by saying, "I have 7,000 prophets who are on reserve, those who have not bowed to Baal."

God was saying, he had a remnant of people who obey Him no matter what. I know some men and women, young and old people, who have remained celibate. Oh to be kept by Jesus.

In 1 Corinthians 7:1, Paul tells the men, it is good not to have a sexual relationship with a woman. But to avoid fornication that will land you in the lake of fire, it's better to get a wife, saints. Or ladies, get a husband. Because living celibate is a very hard thing to do, many people fall back into sin. You have to stand boldly and say, "I will not be defeated by the enemy."

Jesus caused me to be free by dying on Calvary. It's going to work out. Stay in God's Word, get before the Lord and say, "I need thee every hour."

There are going to be some lonely nights and some long days, but remember He has shortened the days for the elect's sake (Matt 24:22).

Think about the person you look up to in the church. The people who really love and fear the Lord. They would all be lost if it wasn't for the days being shortened. That includes Barbara Mitchell. You should be glad He has shortened the days for your sake. Please understand, sin is powerful. Lust has been around for a long time, and it will be here until Jesus' return.

Remember, you are the elect. God pulled a curve ball on the devil. God said, "I will cause the days to be shortened, because no one would be saved if it was the way it was." (Mark 13:20)

So stop saying, "I wish it was the way it used to be."

The devil is not playing fair, but he is trying to pull everybody down. Therefore, you need to thank God for shorter days.

I remember when my daughter was just starting her teen years. She was about 14 years old in her first year in high school, and there was a great deal of pressure about her being celibate.

She would always come home from school and say, "Momma, everybody is having sex or so it seems. It wouldn't be so bad, but the girls are pressuring me to have sex. They are calling me names because I'm not sexually active."

I sat my daughter down, and I explained to her. Most people are not happy with the choices they made in life. Instead of beating up on themselves, they try to make you feel bad. They know the choices they made were wrong. They will go and tease others in order for others to do what they did, so they won't feel alone. We call it peer pressure.

Even the church children will tease other children at church because they are virgins. Can you believe that? Well, believe it. Our children are facing pressure at school and even at church. You may ask, did my daughter listen and apply these words of wisdom to her life? Inquiring minds want to know, but that's her testimony. I will let her tell you. However, I told her the truth. Tell your children the truth about this demon, pray and let God handle the rest.

When I was growing up, it was a disgrace to even mention that someone was having sex before marriage. Sure, some girls in the restroom always discussed sex, but "nice girls" didn't hang with their kind. Now, it's the popular thing to have sex.

You are an outcast if you are 16 and have not had sex—especially boys. Don't be pressured. Get away, fast. Start hanging around positive people, who really love the Lord. God said, "If you love me, keep my commandments."

Therefore, you need to hang around some young people who are sold out for the Lord. If you cannot find them, please pray and ask God to send you a true friend. I'm not saying don't associate with people who are having sex. However, I'm saying be careful who you hang out with. Let God lead you. Ask God to "please order your steps." He will! We do not live by the law, but we walk by faith.

Jesus said, "I didn't come to destroy the law but to fulfill it." (Matt 5:17) He left the Holy Spirit with us so we can obey God and work in His will.

I told my daughter to stand up and be different. I shared with my daughter that sex was a good thing! Yes, Yes, Yes. However, God created it for marriage between male and female. I told her to keep herself for her husband. My friend, you see the devil messed it up with God, and now, he's trying to get you messed up with God.

He wants you to fall just as he did. He is using the lady that sits on his back in order to deceive you. It's serious, my friend. Not only will he try to convince a child to fall like he did my child, but he will convince you and me as adults to fall, if we allow him.

The Bible says, "Resist the devil and he will flee from you." (James 4:7)

When those thoughts come into your mind, just tell the devil, "I will not bow to your evil plots. I will not obey my flesh. This body belongs to the Lord. I'm God's child."

Now pray. Get on your face and cry out to God for strength and help because He's waiting and listening. Now after you have prayed, don't go and call the devil. How do I know that person is being used by the devil? When he or she starts talking out of the will of God, hang up the phone.

If you're at someone's house, you need to go home. Get out of his or her face and leave. Remember—we as humans want what we can't have. I believe if God said you all can have sex like the animals with whomever you choose, whenever you choose, we wouldn't want sex.

The excitement of disobeying God causes our flesh to want to go against His will. I strongly believe sex would not be a problem among humans if we weren't a race that loved to do forbidden things. When you were single, you thought sex was the world with your boyfriend. As soon as you got married, then you didn't want sex like you did before marriage. Why? It's legal with God now. This is how the interest goes outside the marriage. I'm telling you this is so powerful because never have I seen it before like I do today.

Can't you see preachers, teachers, politicians, lawyers, doctors, blue collar workers, white-collar workers, women, men, and children being turned out by the tail? Please open your eyes to see what the devil is doing. He is playing you like a deck of cards.

Is there anybody listening? He has played this game over and over again. I come to expose the devil and this woman. They are using the power of sex to bring you down.

My mind is telling me no, but my body is telling me yes. Who are you going to follow, your body or the spirit of God? The Holy Ghost is saying no. Yes, you may be hot, but go take a cold bath or shower. Now, tell your body this is the Lord's temple. Call someone quickly to pray with you. Don't call the person who is the center of your lust. Call on Jesus. If you can't get a prayer through, confess your fault one to another.

Get another Christian who is strong in the Lord, and tell them to pray the devil right out of your head. Remember, resist the devil and he will flee from you. (James 4:7)

Warning! Be very careful who you tell. There are so many fake Christians. Please pray before you say anything to anybody. No, you don't need sex. You need the Lord, so ask God to help you.

If you give in to the sexual demon, you are back at square one again. You are going to have to conquer this thing, right now. Put a stop to the unsatisfying feeling you are having. For you see, if you don't put a stop to it now, then it will overtake you. The Bible says hell is never satisfied (Habakkuk 2:5, Isaiah 5:14). As I said before, if you don't conquer this demon, it will conquer you.

You will get married and have a cheating spouse or a spouse who is not satisfying you like he or she was prior to getting married. Then the devil will come in like a flood, trying to get you to turn back.

So if you are in the valley of dissatisfaction, then ask God to come and fill the void. Ask Him to save you right now from your fleshly desires. He will do it. Don't you dare get married only for the purpose of saying you are trying to please God. If you can't please Him now, take it from me, it will be far worse if you get married. Because the tests of life are going to come upon you like never before. You are going to either fall for another person or fall in the arms of Christ. It's either now or later.

Don't be ashamed or embarrassed because you are having sexual desires. Ask God to clean, purge, and wash you. He will do it. Yes, I know you will have people saying all types of things about you. You are carnal and you don't pray enough. I don't care how long you pray or cry out to God. There are going to be some lonely moments, and I'm telling you now to tell God the truth. He already knows how you truly feel. Tell him all about it, because he's listening and waiting on you. Deal with it. Don't try to cover it but be open with yourself and say, "God, I need you right now." You will be able to stand my brother, my sister and declare the work of the Lord.

CHAPTER 8

My Wake-Up Call

Remember one incident when I met a lady on the plane and she was from Kenya. I love to talk to my native people. She asked me what I did for a living, and I told her. She said she wanted me to meet her nephew, because he was in the business in Africa, and he wanted to get into the music industry in America.

I met him at the baggage claim, and when I shook his hand a feeling went off in me that I really can't explain. But I knew something was not right at all. When I touched his hand, I was immediately attracted to him.

Please keep in mind that first of all, I'm married. And second, if I wasn't' married, he was not my type at all. When this harlot woman is involved, she will blindside you. Well, that was a sip of the mother of harlots' wine. I was not drunk yet but I had a sip or a taste of what she had to offer. I should have referred him to one of my male producers, but Mrs. Holy here said to herself, "Oh its nothing, I'll do it."

I gave him a copy of my video, and he loved the song "Lord, Make Me Real."

Out of all the songs he could choose, "Lord, Make Me

Real" was his favorite. Funny, how it was also my favorite song. We met each week, and the more I sipped on that lust juice, the drunker I got, until I could not think straight.

Finally, I was getting ready to give it up, if you know what I mean. Yes, I was ready to give everything up for a minute of romance. I mean a hot and steamy romance. For you see in life, you will meet all types of people. But there will come a time when someone crosses your path, and it will feel like you had known that person. This man was that someone, so the harlot had me thinking!

My friends, this was not just an attraction, but it was as if it was a magnet. I had never felt this way before. It was so powerful I expressed my concerns about how powerful this attraction was. Now, I know it was the web of lust. It had finally trapped me again, and I was entangled inside.

How was I going to get out of this?

It seemed as if I was sinking in quicksand, but thank God for Jesus. I called my prayer partners and let them know how I felt. They talked some sense to me until I sobered up. Don't think you can play with the mother of harlots. The MOH (mother of harlots) has been around for a long time. She is powerful.

I stopped meeting with him, and I came out of that situation, victorious without giving it up. Thank you Jesus. But I quickly learned, you cannot beat her on your own. You need the power of God by putting on the whole armor of God so that you may be able to stand against the wiles of the devil.

Pass your test. It's only a test.

After avoiding the trap set before me and overcoming

temptation, I learned some devastating news that was occurring in my own household.

My husband was CHEATING. Right, like I didn't know. All those lies he told me. I still was blind. Not only did he cheat, he fathered a child while married to me. We had been married for 16 plus years, and this child was 11 years old. (Wasn't that amazing?) I remember, when I caught my husband with another woman, and a week later he was in ICU for three weeks. I knew something was wrong but could not quite put my finger on it. God exposed the dark secrets that had been hidden. I was told all about the women who had an affair with my husband for over 12 years and the 11-year-old son he fathered as a result of the affair.

I was so upset I wanted to go back to what I used to do. I wanted to pay him back.

I kept hearing, "Vengeance is mine," says the Lord. (Isa 63:4)

I looked at my husband's present state. His pancreas exploded. Oh it was awful. He almost died. He was laying there in pain. Yes, I prayed he would get better. I told God to forgive him and I forgave him. Even after receiving a call from one of his lovers for over 12 years, I still had the love of Jesus in my heart.

Thank God for Jesus! No, it was not me, it WAS THE LOVE OF JESUS!

She called late one night and said, "I'm in love with your husband." She began to tell me all about their long relationship. The first thing that came to my mind was how stupid I was for erasing the African's number.

God told me to erase the number and the email address, so I would no longer meet with the African guy. And I obeyed. But in the moment, I almost wished I kept some trace of the man.

What are you saying Barbara? As I mentioned before, the Red Sea experience was a seal for the children of Israel. By throwing his information away, I sealed the deal. God not only closed the path to Egypt to keep Pharaoh from getting to the children of Israel, he also closed the path of the Red Sea so the children of Israel wouldn't go back to Egypt. The scriptures say they wanted to go back when they were in the wilderness, saying what they had in Egypt was better than their present state (Ex. 14:12)

God is saying, "Don't look back. Keep moving ahead. Destiny is straight ahead!"

Yes, my friend, God is saying to you right now; erase the numbers and the email addresses. Change your number. When the devil comes in and tries to justify you going back, you will not be able to go back to Egypt. Don't turn back. God will keep you even when you don't want to be kept. He closed up the

Red Sea for their sake. He loved you enough to close up your Red Sea.

You must forget those things, which are behind and press toward the mark of the high calling which is in Christ Jesus." The devil and this harlot are after you. I know they have your spouse, friends, maybe your pastor. But don't let him have you.

You are on an assignment. Don't let that tail bring you down. Wound the devil. Cut him loose.

Don't Let "*The Tail*" Bring You Down

Isaiah 51:9 says, "Awake, awake, put on strength, O arm of the Lord awake, as in the ancient days, in generation of old. Art thou not it that hath cut Rahab, and wounded the dragon?

Do you know who Rahab was? She helped the spies Joshua sent over to spy out the promise land. Rahab was a harlot. She worked for the MOH. But Rahab switched sides. I heard someone say, "Instead of laying down with the men, Rehab lifted them up onto the roof of her house. For this reason, her family and she was saved. Instead of sleeping with them, she helped them with the will of the Lord. When she lifted the men of God up, instead of lying down with them, Rahab wounded the devil. She actually cut the dragon.

Please understand, when you cut the devil loose, you hurt the "Dragon." He feels it when you change sides.

Change sides today. Lift that pastor or musician up in prayer right now. Go to the back of the book and begin to write the prayers down for each person you are attracted to. Lift them up in prayer. Cut the devil. Cut him loose. I know you have worked for them a long time.

Cut him! Cut her!

I'm not saying cut them physically, but cut them spiritually. When you physically cut loose from the sins you are in, it spiritually cuts the dragon, and then you cut the transportation the MOH rides upon. You know she is riding on the back of the beast, which is the devil, you messed with her ride. It's like a broken-down vehicle. She cannot get very far.

Are you wondering how you can get vengeance on the

devil? Cut him loose, and you will wound him BAD!

Memorize Rev 18:4-8 that says, "Come out of her my people, that ye be not partakers of her sins, and that ye receive not of her plagues. Cut her loose

Reward her even as she rewarded you, and double unto her double according to her works and the cup which she hath filled fill to her double. How much she hath glorified herself, and lived deliciously, so much torment and sorrow give her: for she saith in her heart, I sit a queen, and am no widow, and shall see no sorrow. Therefore, shall her plagues come in one day, death, and mourning, and famine; and she shall be utterly burned with fire for strong is the Lord God who judgeth her."

Cut her or him today! Don't wait another minute or an hour. Do it right now in Jesus name.

You cannot fight what you cannot see, so get into the spirit. The spirit will show you what the devil and this woman are plotting.

> *"For the flesh lusteth against the Spirit, and the Spirit against the flesh: and these are contrary the one to the other: so that ye cannot do the things that ye would."*
> *(Galatians 5:17)*

Perhaps you want vengeance right now, but the Bible says, "Vengeance is mine saith the Lord." (Roman 12:19)

Your spouse may have been caught red-handed, but you have to get into a secret place and pray. You don't have to be on your knees. Wherever you are reading this book, just stop and pray. Get into the Spirit. You don't have to close your eyes, just pray in your heart. God will hear you. No it's not fair and yes you don't understand but you will understand it better by and by. For now get to know Jesus better. This is an opportunity to get closer to God. This is a chance to fall into his arms. I'm telling you he has his arms open wide.

I don't care how big your sins are. He is able to save you. Do it now.

CHAPTER 9

Don't Lose Your Position

Several of our leaders lost or almost lost their position, and some lost their respect because of the tail. The third of the angels lost their position because of the tail as well.

Not only did Satan lose his position, but he drew a third of the angelic host out of Heaven with his tail. One would say angels know nothing about the tail or sexual sins.

Gen 6:2 That the sons of God saw the daughters of men that they [were] fair; and they took them wives of all which they chose. This verse proves angels know about sex. As I stated before concerning Gen 6:2. Angels had SEX with humans. No, they weren't supposed to have sex with humans, but they did. God was angry because sin had covered the earth. We as humans are the same. When it comes to our sexual desires, always wanting to go against the Word of the Lord.

The ANGELS knew about sexual sins. This thing is so deep. I'm telling you just read the Word for yourself and you will see. Sexual immorality is powerful. These sinful acts caused God to regret making man. As a result, Noah and his family were the only ones who were saved from the flood.

There were angels who were thrown out of Heaven because of the tail. Rev 12:4 – 12:8. Angels lost their position, their Heavenly homes only to follow the tail. Read the Word.

I know you are saying it's not that easy to stop cold turkey. Well you better, before you lose everything you have. Don't let anyone tell you, "Well, I fall into sin all the time, and I still have my position." Or "I'm still getting closer and closer to God."

My friends, don't be fooled. The farther you are from God, the less you will hear his voice.

Then you will eventually lose the power that works in you. You will not be as strong to fight against the enemy, and you will lose the position God placed you in. He has ordained you to do His will, not whatever you will.

Jesus prayed, "Father Thy will be done, not my will."

Yes, you may still have the position with man, but you have lost the position with God. Don't let the tail bring you down. I know you can sing really well or you can preach really well. It might seem you have not lost any anointing. Maybe people are falling out when you minister.

In spite of all of that, you have been replaced. Look at King Saul in the Old Testament. Even though Saul remained the current king, God had already anointed another king. Saul didn't realize the anointing had left him, and God had already replaced him. If you don't repent, you will be replaced. (Repent or be replaced.) Now please note, the Bible points out Saul disobeying God. It doesn't say Saul had sexual sins. However, my point is, when you disobey God you could be in danger of losing everything you work so hard to have.

You are on your way to HELL and will be thrown into the lake of fire if you don't repent! No excuses. Please understand, Saul killed himself with his own sword (1Sam 31:4). The devil cannot stop you or kill you. He can only convince you to destroy yourself. Don't commit suicide. Don't take someone else's life. It's not that bad. The enemy will have you so far out there that you can't see your way back.

Hold on to what you know and repent. God will bring you back man or woman of God. You belong to God!

Don't let anyone tell you that you can keep sinning, and God will keep forgiving you for that same sin over and over.

Shall we continue in sin? Romans 6:2 answers the question. God forbid. By no means are we to continue doing wrong. When you are truly ready, you will repent and put it down once and for all.

Ask God for his divine help. You have to have a mind to do this, but ask God for help because you can't do it on your own. We must admit that it's too strong for us.

I remember asking God over and over when I was in sin and finally God spoke to me. And He said, "Barbara, I've given you chance after chance, and you continue."

He told me to give Him my life, and I did. The change wasn't overnight. It took some time and changes in my life that I will talk about later on. But it can be done.

My brothers and sisters, sin is controlled by the devil and the mother of harlots. It seems as if a large percentage of the world has been sipping on her lust juices. When you look in our churches, we see divorce rates are higher than ever. Look at the nations everywhere, not just in the USA, but I'm talking about everywhere.

Now the going words are just follow your feelings wherever they may take you.

"Just do what you feel is right." Every feeling that you had in the past, present, or future is not the right feeling. 1 John 4:1 says; "Beloved, believe not every spirit, but try the spirits whether they are of God: because many false prophets are gone out into the world."

You have to try the spirits and see if it's of God. Do not follow the way you feel if it's biblically wrong.

It's just like a child when he or she is small wanting the latest toy displayed on TV. When that child is older, they do not feel the same way about the toy when they were younger. In most cases, your feelings will change.

Do not do whatever feels right or whatever you desire to do. Jesus said, "Father, not my will but thou will be done".

Resist Satan and this woman. If you feel like you just got to have this person, but you know it's wrong, just say no. God has better things in store for you, if you just hold on.

From this day forward, stop sipping off of her lust juice. It makes you drunk, and a drunken person is not aware of the decisions they make. It's only when they become sober do they realize how stupid they were. I'm telling you the best way is God's way. Listen, it's just like the saying, "Don't drive drunk if you know you are tipsy."

Call a friend, a safe, delivered friend to help you get away. Make sure this friend will pray you through, not cause you to sin more. Call a prayer partner, Make sure they are Spirit-filled. Ask God to come into your life and clean up everything that needs to be cleaned up. He can and will do it if you ask.
You don't have to stay where you are.

Revelation 18:4-5 says, "And I heard another voice from Heaven, saying, Come out of her, my people, that ye be not partakers of her sins, and that ye receive not of her plagues. For her sins have reached unto heaven, and God hath remembered her iniquities."

Again, I repeat come out of her. This is an appeal to every preacher, teacher, evangelist, deacon, musician, singer, church helper, and members of the body of Christ. The bridegroom is soon to come, so don't be unprepared.

Many people think if they accepted Jesus one time and just believe, everything will be alright. I have my light now, and it's shining. Please don't think just because you give Jesus your heart this is all you must do. Faith without works is dead, and works without faith is dead (James 2:17). It's a daily walk with God. You cannot do whatever you want to do and say Jesus is Lord over your life. It's not your life anyway, so why are you trying to please the body. It will never be satisfied no matter what. So live for God with all your heart. It's His body. Our bodies are God's temple. Make sure the temple is clean saints.

Galatians 5:16-19 says, "This I say then Walk in the Spirit, and ye shall not fulfill the lust of the flesh. For the flesh lusted against the Spirit, and the Spirit against the flesh: and these are contrary the one to the other: so that ye cannot do the things that ye would. But if ye be led of the Spirit, ye are not under the law Now the works of the flesh are manifest, which are these: adultery, fornication, uncleanness, lasciviousness."

For the flesh lusteth against the Spirit, and the Spirit against the flesh: and these are contrary the one to the other, so that ye cannot do the things that ye would (Gal 5:17). They are in conflict with each other, so that you do not do everything you want. You may want it really bad, but the Spirit of God says don't give into the flesh.

"The Wages of sin is death and the gift of God is eternal life."
(Romans 6:23)

Don't die trying to get a feel good. So many people have contracted so many diseases as well as been killed trying to commit sinful acts. The payoff is eventually death. Is it worth losing your life? I think not. Let's talk about the woman who rides the dragon's back. She is a hunter. She finds the prey, and she hunts them down. To understand her hunting ability we must first look at female lions. The Bible says, in 1 Pet 5:8, "the devil is as a roaring lion."

The devil roars like the male lion, and the mother of harlots hunts like the female lion. The female lion brings the food for her entire family even to the male lion.

Just imagine the conversation between the devil and her.

"Didn't I tell you I would get them? No, money could not get them, lying couldn't get them, gambling—nothing could conquer them. But I will get them through lust and pride.

"When I place the lust into their spirits, they will be too proud to say I need help. They will be too proud to go and get into the prayer line, because they are ministers, pastors, and teachers. They will be too proud to tell their friends, I need help in dealing with lust."

A very high percentage of those in church praying for you are bound by the spirit of lust themselves. This is the way the spirits travel and they are getting worse among God's people, because they are being transferred by some of the altar workers. They are giving into the flesh saying, "The spirit is willing, but the flesh is weak." Repent today.

I know her bed is sweet. There is nothing like SEX! How it can make you feel. And for some reason when you are cheating, it feels soooooo good.

Well, it's all in your head. I know he or she makes you feel like no other. They don't realize they are being used. The Blood of Jesus against you Satan!

When a person is cheating, it feels like everything the other person is saying sounds so good or whatever they are doing seems to be so good. The mood is always right. I know her underclothes always match, and she always smells incredible. He or she always thinks of the right things to say. The words come just when you need to hear them. He smells wonderful. Then at your weakest moment, he or she will say "Just let your feelings go, and go with the flow."

STOP! RUN!

When your mind is running to and fro, the devil has you in the valley of decision. You are wondering in the wilderness of your mind saying, "I want to but I shouldn't do it."

What do you do now? Run! Run like Joseph ran. I pray your eyes become open now. The devil is out to kill and destroy. That other person does not think you're the best lover in the world. I know it seems as if no one can touch you quite the same as he or she can. When you know you can't have something, this is a fight all by itself.

I don't know why this human body loves to have challenges. Instead of obeying the flesh, you need to press past this test. You may have failed several times, but press.

Jesus died that we might have the victory. If they shall fall away, to renew them again unto repentance; seeing they crucify to themselves the Son of God afresh, and put him to an open shame. (Hebrew 6:6)

Don't put Jesus back on the cross. You have the power now. Access the Holy Ghost inside of you. Let the spirit take control.

Let me pray with you.

Father I come to you standing in agreement with _____ (your name). I pray right now for my brother or my sister. I know you said to come boldly to your throne, so now we come boldly but humbly, asking you to touch his or her body. You made us and you know all about the situation. Right now touch my brother or sister. We need your help to fight the enemy inside our minds. Thank you for this precious gift that you have given us as mortal men and women called sex, to enjoy as married couples. However, Lord, we need your help to control this desire and use it for the right reason. Help us to use the precious gift of sex for which you designed between the husband and the wife only. The blood of Jesus against the devil and this woman who rides on the back of the beast. You have no place in this holy temple. Now I command you to leave in the name of Jesus. We pray, AMEN.

Now I want you to repeat after me. I'm free, I'm free, I'm free!

CHAPTER 10

Let Her Go
"The Mother of Harlot"

T rust me it is hard to let her go after being under the influence for so many years. It's going to take the Holy Spirit to intervene on your behalf.

I know personally what you are going through. For you see, throughout this book, I have shared only a portion of my testimony with you. Let me tell you how it all began.

I was once in her family. For years, I let her control me. She told me I needed a man, and I needed him now.

I believed her!

She told me I could not make it without a man. I needed to have sex all day, every day. Soon after I started having sex, I could not stop.

At first, I was not having sex to feel good. I was having sex to get what I could out of boys and men. As a matter of fact, my first sexual experience was with a boy I didn't even like. My sister, dated his friend and asked me to have sex with her boyfriend's friend who liked me. I was young and stupid and said ok. Dumb.com right? I know, but I didn't know any better.

Later on, that same boy I had sex with would have tokens for the video games. So guess what stupid, young, dumb me said. OK. I'm going to get some tokens from him, or he will buy my food.

After a while, I graduated to making guys buy me clothes or jewelry, and soon my taste became larger and larger for sex exchanges. It went on and on until I became obsessed with it. If you recall from Revelation 17:4, which we read and explained at the beginning of this book, many women and men are not having sex for the feeling. They are committing sexual sin to get their bills paid or to buy the latest fashions. Proverbs tells us they are being "arrayed in purple scarlet." I know the devil and your spiritual momma is saying you need him or her to pay your <u>bills or whatever</u> (you fill in blank), or you need him or her to have a confidante.

Everybody knows that sex is often used to get a promotion and monetary gain, etc. Let me make this clear before I go any further. I never used sex to get a solo part or a song on a cd or anything else dealing with my career. Thank God.

However, it does happen. We all know this goes on in the secular world. But I'm sorry to say it also often takes place within the church. Even though I didn't sleep around for a song or a position in the gospel industry, what I did before I was married for my bills, clothes and jewelry was basically the same thing.

It is amazing how this woman, which I call lust, will cause you to feel as if you really need a new pair of shoes or a new car or even that promotion. She will cause you to feel you need your light, cable and phone bill paid and there is no other way.

You don't need the new furniture. I know it seems more important than pleasing God. However, get your mind back. Go buy your own things. Revelation 17 indicates that she loves nice things, and she will have you behaving like a prostitute.

Truly, I'm not saying that every man or woman who loves nice things belongs to her. What I am saying is that if you have to commit fornication or adultery to get those nice things, then you belong to her. (That's yo momma.) She is very much in control of your life. Yes, I will say it again. She is your mother. I know this is not your desire.

Just because you are not on the local corner does not mean you are not a prostitute. I was a materialistic prostitute by way of the church. Oh don't get deep with me. There are so many prostitutes in the church, male and female. The prostitutes on the local corner, or the call girls, are getting money for their services. And what are you getting?

The car payment, lights, cable bills, and sometimes nothing but the satisfaction to say I was with that significant other? You are still a prostitute, and the mother of harlots is still your mother.

Repent today. Do it now, before it's too late. He is married and wants you to be his side kick. His wife doesn't care. Please remember God does care! Don't be fooled, people of God. Repent today!

Later on, during my 11th grade year in high school, I went to the dentist to get a tooth pulled. Little did I know I would meet a man who would change my life forever.

First, he asked me to work for him part-time. At the time, I already had a part-time job at the library, but I said yes. Knowing he was over 40, I saw what he had to offer. He let me drive his Mercedes to school. Everybody looked up to me.

Finally, he made his move, and I didn't resist at all. I kind of liked the fact he wanted a little country girl, because he was a "city man." I didn't know this would be the beginning of a materialistic journey that would last a long time.

During this time, I was not faithful to him. I continued to date over the years and have sex with many guys without him knowing. I didn't know how to be faithful.

One night I caught the dentist with another woman. I cried and asked why. He assured me it was nothing. Even though I was cheating, I was deeply hurt to see he was doing the same thing.

Do you see how stupid I was? Getting mad at him for cheating, yet knowing I had been cheating all along. After this incident, I became buck wild as one would say. I cared nothing about anyone's feelings but my own. For you see, deep inside I did care a great deal about this man. However, I didn't know how to be faithful.

Thanks be unto God, who kept me even when I didn't know any better. By the way, while I'm on this subject, I would like to sincerely apologize to everybody I hurt. I'm very sorry for my foolish and selfish actions. To all who I caused to stop trusting women, I'm sorry from the bottom of my heart. All those years, I thought I was playing those guys, but the mother of harlots was playing me the whole time. I was a church girl, but that's all—just a girl who attended church. I didn't have church inside of me.

This behavior was not learned from my father and mother, because they were true believers, and they set a perfect example. I know the devil and this mother of harlots knew the calling on my life, and knew I would bless many people through my ministry. So they set out to destroy me before I got to my destiny. You see, this woman doesn't require you to fill out an application or send a resume. She looks for whoever will work for her. Let them come. Pretty, ugly, fat, skinny, or fine, all are welcome. She does not care because she wants you to work for her.

Growing up, I was a perfect seven and everything was in the right place. You could not tell me I wasn't fine. No one did, because it was a fact that I was fine.

Let me paint the picture for you. I remember walking down my college hallway during the first week of school. I had on a yellow outfit I bought from an expensive store with some man's money. The suit fit my body so perfectly that when I walked through the main hallway, many members of the basketball team at the college stopped, stared and some fell down saying how fine I was.

It went directly to my head, and I was so embarrassed I didn't wear that suit again until the end of the school year. No, I didn't have sex with any of the basketball players. I believed it was not proper to date anybody who attended the same home church or school. But I had my share of men in other places.

Once I thought I was doing well by letting some guys

go when the preacher preached about hell. I wanted to make it right with God. So instead of being with ten men, I only had three. I thought I was so in love with the top three. It sounds so stupid to me now. We all know when you are in love, you only should think about the ONE you love. Right? The mother of harlots had me so senseless I believed I was in love with all three guys.

Believe it or not, I prayed every night before I went to bed—even after I would have sex.

I would be in the bed saying, "God forgive me for my sins."

I knew I was hurting God, but didn't want to stop having sex. If you would have asked me back then, I would have told you I was deeply in love with God as well.

I want to know what love is. Love is action. But I didn't show action behind closed doors. Oh in church, I loved God. I wouldn't do what the "worldly people did," but I was screwing every night. (The blood of Jesus against that demon). I couldn't stop. It was too good, and I was having so much fun. So I thought. I was addicted. Revelation 17:6 says she is drunk on the blood of the saints. It felt like she was a vampire sucking the life right out of me.

By now, it had gotten so bad that I remember standing in line waiting for some food I ordered, and there was a nice-looking young man. I winked at him, and he asked my name. I told him, and we talked for a minute.

Then I whispered to my sister, "I think I want him."

She thought I was saying I wanted to talk to him, but I wanted to have sex with him right then and there.

I had a spirit in me that believed I could get anybody I wanted. Yes. The same night I had sex with him, and I didn't even know his name. I dated him for a while, until I found out he had a nice car but didn't have any money. I was like the harlot in Proverbs 7 at this time. The only difference was that she was married, and I wasn't. When I was single, I always believe I shouldn't mess with married men. Thank God for the convictions. If I found out a man was married, then I would not bother with him at all. At that time, I just could not even think about dating another woman's husband. So you can relax women. No one I experienced sex with was married. I don't know if I thought I would win brownie points with God for this, but that was in my do not policy book.

Despite all the other stuff I did, God still kept me. Praise the Lord! You better believe if I had not gotten married, that harlot would have had me dating married men and women. For you see, sin has you going to places you never intended to go.

As the years went by, I felt like I was running out of time. I was 19 years old and had graduated with an Associate's degree. I had no real relationship, so I turned to drinking. Now, the devil said, "Kill yourself."

I started to after my last abortion that I will talk about later. Someone was always there to interrupt the overdose. Thanks be unto God.

You see, they work hand and hand—sex, alcohol and drugs. The devil and the mother of harlots will cause you to start drinking alcohol and using drugs.

Let me let you in on their scheme. She convinces you

to do all these things, and then the devil plays with your emotions. So you can take your own life, because now you are humiliated.

He knew he could not destroy me, so he told me to destroy myself. You must know the devil and this mother of harlots is trying to stop you. He wants you dead. He wants your name, fame and reputation. He wants your name attached to bad news, so your witness will not be effective. I'm telling you they are using you. I know, because for years they used me.

If you are being used by the devil and the mother of harlots, then pray this prayer now:

Lord, I have sinned against You and Your kingdom. Lord, I'm sorry. Forgive me and take complete control of my Life. Take away the ungodly desires, the pride, the guilt and the shame. Please take it away. Amen.

Now, take a moment and cry out to God. Thank him for deliverance.

As I said before, I felt like I was running out of time, because I became involved with guys I didn't even want. It seemed like I needed to have sex three times a day. I behaved in this manner, because I didn't like myself. In public it wasn't noticeable, but when I got home, I hated not receiving a phone call.

When I didn't receive a phone call from anyone, the devil would whisper in my ears and say, "No one wants you anymore. You will never get married, and you are too fat now. "As I mentioned before, weight was not a problem. The mother of harlots would point out all of my weaknesses, so then I would call someone to prove to her I had what it took to have someone in my bed. It was like a battle inside of my head, and they were winning.

After I had sex, it was like I was saying, "Now, who's in control."

Yes, she played me like a deck of cards.

After I would do these things, fear would set up in my heart. I was so scared God was coming to get me, and I knew I was not ready. I would have nightmares that Jesus came back, and the world was on fire, and I was saying, "Lord, give me one more chance."

I remember sitting in my mother's living room after we had a great time at church and an airplane was flying low. I thought that was Gabriel's trumpet. Now, I know it was the spirit of God calling me to turn to Him. But even then I didn't listen.

The next week I was back at church again. The Spirit of God used me to sing mightily and people were falling out under the anointing and jumping everywhere. I also felt good, and I even jumped and praised God.

Soon after the benediction, I felt like I needed some sex. I should have pleaded the blood of Jesus. The scariest part is that when the church service was over and after the spirit was very high; I would feel the need to have sex. So each time the Spirit of God would move on my heart to change me, MOH would come back even stronger to possess me.

After church, she convinced me I could not go to sleep unless I had someone next to me. As a result, I slept with so many men. Thank God he has redeemed me! I was stupid because I yielded to her every time. That enemy knew I had an anointing over my life, and it wanted to destroy me. The enemy knew what I liked and what I didn't like. That spirit was so powerful.

But I gave the enemy power!

I remember being so sexually active I thought my life was on the line. Thank you God I got out just in time. The year I got married, people started contracting AIDS in full force, but to God be the glory, I was not infected. I should have had AIDS, but thanks be unto God. I'm AIDS free. Thank you Jesus. Even with a cheating husband, I still didn't get infected. Thank you Jesus!

I regretfully admit I had three abortions. I feel so bad about how I let the devil use me.

As I stated, I wanted to kill myself because I felt God didn't love me for having those abortions. I am so thankful I heard a preacher say, "God will forgive you for all sins if you repent."

I repented and never did that again. Thank God for saving me. I apologize to all the young women I talked about and looked down on for having their baby when they weren't married. But I aborted my babies. Not only did I murder three times, I felt I had to do this, and it was okay with God to protect my family. The devil had me out of my mind. I had a reprobate mind. I thought I was doing right by not having a baby, because as I stated before, my father was a pastor, and my mother was a missionary and a prophetess. I felt it would disgrace the family if I had a child and was not married.

I had sisters who were having babies, and they were not married. I saw how it devastated my father and mother, and I never wanted to hurt them—especially my father.

My mother and father would have told me to have that baby, but I didn't want to have it, for I felt it would hurt them.

Trust me. I have asked God to forgive me for this, and I continue to encourage women who didn't make the mistake I did, but instead they had their babies. Thank God they didn't choose the path which I chose. I didn't realize at the time, I was hurting my Heavenly father even.

My daughter became pregnant before she was married. She was going to have an abortion because "I was an evangelist," and she didn't want to bring embarrassment to our ministry. She was also afraid, because she felt she wasn't ready.

She didn't tell me, but she called my sister, Margaree. My sister convinced her to sit down and talk to me. I was so appreciative. I begged her not to make the same mistake I made. Well, I'm so glad she didn't do it.

If you are in this situation or similar to this situation, then please stop to pray this prayer:

Father, I am sorry. I admit that I need your help. Forgive me and renew the right spirit in me. Father save me. Let your Holy Spirit take control of my life. Thank you father that you are now beginning a new work in me. In Jesus Name Amen.

Don't kill your baby. Have that precious child. My

sisters had their children, and now most of their children are active in church, doing the work of the Lord. Don't be a fool like I was. Accept your responsibilities, and go ahead and have the child.

I'm not saying it was right that you had sex without being married, but I am saying you should not try to cover up your mistake like I did.

David tried to cover up his sins. He slept with Bathsheba, and she became pregnant. Her husband Uriah was in the military. He was a warrior fighting for his country and loyal to his God and King David. David called for Uriah to come home.

He came home, however he didn't have sex with his wife. After several failed attempts, David decided to put him on the frontline and told the leader of the warriors to pull back. He wanted Uriah dead to cover up his affair with Bathsheba.

Don't try to cover your sins. Ask God to forgive you and to give you a new start. I thank GOD He saved me and filled me with the precious Holy Ghost. Now it's for real. Thanks be to GOD, it's for real.

This is a spirit, so you must get in the spirit to fight the spirit. You are going to have to conquer this thing. Put a stop to the demonic feeling you are having.

You may say, "I just can't get enough of sex, I just can't stop."

Yes you can, ask God to help you. He will do it!

CHAPTER 11

Joseph Stood
"What about You"

You may be wondering, "How do I overcome this demon? " To answer this question, let's go to the Word of God. Joseph is a prime example to the body of Christ.

In Genesis 39, he ran from Potiphar's wife, (even though she was beautiful and his job was on the line). He stood for what was right. So many women and men think, if they don't sleep with their boss or leaders (who are in charge), they will not get the promotion or monetary gain.

In Joseph's situation the devil tried to make it seem as if Potiphar's wife was his meal ticket out of his situation.

HE REFUSED TO DISOBEY GOD!

When Joseph made the right decision, Joseph was accused of attempted rape and thrown in a lonely jail. Later on in the story, he became Potiphar's boss. Pharaoh made him second in charge of his entire kingdom. (Gen 41:41)

The devil wants you to think, if you go ahead and have the affair with that married man or woman, all your financial needs will be met. You will not have to worry about anything. All your troubles will be over. Well, I come to tell you that if you give in to the devil, you have not seen anything like the kind of trouble that will come your way sooner or later. I know someone told you it's okay to have a married woman or man. Some even say they enjoy having someone else's spouse, because the cheating spouse tries extra hard to keep the relationship with their side kick. Meaning they try to give them whatever they want.

This might be true. However, eventually they move on to someone else or they leave the wife and some marry again only to cheat again. All this drama is a trap. Don't let the devil fool you. He is using you to bring down someone's soul to eternal damnation. Remember when you stand before the throne, you are going to have to answer to God for your evil actions. Remember, what goes around comes back around.

You are hell bound, and you are taking someone else with you. I know it seems as if you are not getting ahead. Your living is not in vain. Don't worry. God will raise you up. Don't compromise with the enemy. Promotion comes from God (1Pet 5:6).

When Potiphar's wife made a pass at Joseph, he could have taken the easy road out by just sleeping with her. When she threatened to tell, he said he didn't want to upset God.

In this day and time there are some church leaders who are always telling you about how David messed up. Yes, David sinned against God, but there is someone <u>who made a stand</u> for righteousness, even in the New Testament. There were some people in the Bible that stood for holiness. Joseph refused to have another man's wife. This is why God blessed him later on in the story.

Can GOD trust you? This is a great story for your Single's Ministry. Please read.

And it came to pass after these things, that his master's wife cast her eyes upon Joseph; and she said, lie with me. But he refused, and said unto his master's wife,

Behold, my master wotteth not what is with me in the house, and he hath committed all that he hath to my hand; there is none greater in this house than I: neither hath he kept back anything from me but thee, because thou art his wife: how then can I do this great wickedness, and sin against GOD? (Genesis 39:7-9)

Listen. You must understand that if he had slept with Potiphar's wife, he would have not only sinned against Potiphar, but against God as well.

There was a song we once sang when I was a girl which says "Don't let Jesus down." There should be a level of trust God has in you. Not only trusting in God, but can God trust you? Can he present you to the heavenly host and to the devil saying, "Have you considered my servant _____ (your name)?" (As in Job 1:8).

Job 1:7 tells us, Satan is going to and fro, walking up and down the earth. In 1 Peter 5:8, he is an adversary seeking whom he may devour.

Don't be unwise. The devil wants to kill you and me. Please make up your mind today, just as Joseph did. Do not accept everything offered to you. Joseph wanted to be faithful to God so he "turned sex down." He said no to the temptation. Although the person looks good and it seems like he or she wants you, you must refuse this one. Say yes to God and no to sin.

There is a divine reason you are reading this book. God wants to bless you in a mighty way. I know this is so hard to do, but there is a blessing behind the door when you say "No." God wants to take you to another level in Him. Uphold the name of the Lord Jesus. He is watching you right now.

You have the power to turn him or her down. God is not coming out of the sky to tell you to say no. He has sent me to tell and remind you to REFUSE IT. Resist the devil now in Jesus name. Watch God elevate you higher and higher in the spirit and in the natural.

No they are not your husband. You know you are not married to this man or woman. Just do what is right! You will be exalted in due season. He wants to take you to another level of faith in him. Just trust him. Give him your will and take his will. Don't be a fool! Wake up out of that deep sinful sleep. God does care about your choices. Diligently seek him (Hebrew 11:6). He knows your heart, and this is why he allowed the temptation to come, because he knows you can pass the test.

He will not allow us to be tempted above that we can be tempted (Jam 1:13-14, 1 Cor10:13). If he allowed it to come across your path while traveling on this journey, then you can pass the test. Say no to the flesh, and say yes to the spirit.

Yes, it can be done. Jesus came that you can overcome

this great sin. You have to be alert at all times, and remember God is with you.

So if God is present, will you continue to have sex with a person who's not your spouse? Imagine, every time you have sex, God is in the same room. God is watching you and this individual make love. If you are not married to him or her, you know God is not pleased.

Imagine that individual is Satan with horns or their head. Yeah, you got it. Doesn't this make you have second thoughts about fornicating or committing adultery?

If you said yes, then great. Do you not realize you are in the presence of God almighty? Remember God is everywhere. Yes, even in the dark room with the door closed. God is still there.

Ask yourself a question. Would you have sex in front of the entire church congregation? Then if you will not do this in front of your earthly audience or peers, what about the heavenly Father and the heavenly audience? God knows. He sees everything you do.

The enemy is looking for an easy target. Don't let it be you.

And beheld among the simple ones, I discerned among the youths, a young man void of understanding. Passing through the street near her corner; and he went the way to her house. I have decked my bed with coverings of tapestry, with carved work, with fine linen of Egypt. I have perfumed my bed with myrrh, aloes, and cinnamon.

Come, let us take our fill of love until the morning: let us solace ourselves with loves. For the goodman is not at home, he is gone a long journey; Let not thine heart decline to her ways, go not astray in her paths. For she hath cast down many wounded; yea, many strong men have been slain by her. Her house is the way to hell, going down to the chambers of death. (Proverb 7:7-8, 16-19, 25-27)

Young man void of understand is not talking about age. This is talking about being mature in God. I have seen 75- and 80-year-old men and women who are young in the mind and void of understanding—just plain old foolish.

For all my older readers, you know you don't function like you use to. Give your life to the Lord today. Don't be deceived. They may be beautiful or handsome on the outside but inside, it's pure ugly. They are letting the enemy use them. Don't let him use you. You are blind. Tell God to open your eyes, for you are under the influence of this evil spirit of lust, the mother of harlots. I beg you to get out now.

Perhaps the relationship has been going on for years, and it seems as if you are in love. Ask God for guidance. Don't fall into this trap. Get out while you have time. This is a warning and it's a simple one.

The devil is fooling you. Do not allow him to cause your death in the very act putting you and your family to shame. Don't do it. You young men and women who think you have it going on, you are full of pride, and nobody can tell you anything.

Well you are in a fantasy world. This world will soon turn your life upside down. You don't have a clue what you are getting involved in. Sure you did a background check.

Sure, you know that he or she doesn't have AIDS, but what you don't know is there's a demon trying to destroy your life. If you could see this person now in the spirit, then you would know there is a demonic force in control of you and your sex partner.

Just imagine maggots on the inside of them. Take a look in the spirit, then you will see. Wake up out of your deep sleep. Come to yourself and repent. Jesus loves you.

The Bible says; "I returned, and saw under the sun, that the race is not to the swift, nor the battle to the strong, neither yet bread to the wise, nor yet riches to men of understanding, nor yet favor to men of skill; but time and chance happeneth to them all." (Eccl. 9:11).

Many people are saying, "Hunnie, if you are really in the Lord, you wouldn't even be thinking about a man or woman."

Perhaps sex is not a temptation for them. I'm happy! However, temptation is an enticement.

People who are saying "I don't have those feelings, because I bury my face in the holy book." Good for you. The bible says, "And they overcame them by the blood of the Lamb and by the word of their testimony."

This is my testimony! I'm not ashamed. God brought me out, and I'm going to tell it everywhere I go.

Remember this, man should always pray. Continue to pray. You don't have to ask for temptation. It comes upon you without warning. But know God provides a way of escape if we will accept it (1Corinthians 10:13). Please, never say **N**ever. I pray you say, "Lord, keep me every day." Please have on the full armor of God so you may be able to stand against the wiles of the devil. We wrestle not against flesh and blood but against principalities, against powers, against the rulers of the darkness of this world, against spiritual wickedness in high places. (Ephesians 6:11-12)

You will not believe the number of people who don't reveal their true feelings because of fear that someone might judge them. It is so easy to fall into judging people.

If you are a leader or a minister and someone reveals his or her true feelings to you, then you are not to judge them but to pray for them. Keep it real. If you are having feelings for a married man or woman, then I suggest you ask God to give you an honest and non-judgmental prayer partner, with whom you may confide and you can share your deepest feelings.

Remember the devil desires to sift you as wheat. For you see, preacher, the mother of harlots and the devil wants to make you fall, so you can't preach on sexual sins anymore. And if you do happen to mention it, it is in the last part of the sermon. You only stay on the subject for three seconds.

While I'm on this subject, I want to encourage leaders who are addressing this issue. I want you to know God is pleased with you for preaching the truth. Continue to share the truth, no matter who doesn't like it.

Now, for those leaders who have slipped and fallen, you need to get up! Tell someone, even if you have to call in on a prayer line and don't give your name for right now. I'm telling you to seek God about whom to share this with. Perhaps, you cannot share it with anybody right now. It's alright. And they overcame him by the blood of the Lamb and by the word of their testimony; and they loved not their lives unto death. (Rev 12:11) We are overcomers by the blood of the Lamb and by the words or our testimony.

Eventually, after you talk to God you will be able to tell your testimony to the world. Remember, as long as you keep it on the inside, then sooner or later you will give in to the flesh. It will eat you alive. Now, be really careful how you reveal this to some people. Please be led by God about this. It's ok to tell someone to pray for you. I don't care what position you may hold in the church, you need someone to pray for you.

This is a spirit that is haunting you. MOH will cause you to hit rock bottom. Preachers, teachers, and evangelists, by confessing your faults you will receive the gift of eternal life. Some preachers will not talk about it, because they are involved. You need to pray.

Stop what you are doing, call a prayer line and pray. Don't pray for another person. If you are under the influence of this demonic spirit, then this will transfer into someone else. Don't keep doing wrong and saying God's grace is sufficient. It is sufficient, but God forbids us from continuing to willfully sin.

Yes, this is wickedness. After much prayer, if you are married, I suggest you sit your spouse down and talk to him or her. Make SURE you are led by God first. For most saints, it will remove the power of the mother of harlots and the devil. If you can't go into detail, tell them to pray for you. You all pray together, and watch God work this out.

I remember when I went through my test. My husband

was not a "holy man" and he was still doing some things that didn't please God.

I remember telling him, "Listen, I've been having some unusual feelings. You stay out all night for whatever reason. I have feelings, too.

I love the Lord, but I'm going through some changes."

When I first shared what I was feeling with my husband, he was fine until he got drunk. Then he would bring it up repeatedly. He tormented me with my own words for months and months. Time and time again, he constantly repeated what I had shared with him.

I was so upset, because I did nothing with the African man. I just had a mind to do it, but would not fulfill the lust of the flesh. However, my husband went on and on, night after night, day after day. I asked the Lord; to give me the strength to go through.

Now, he does not bother me, because I caught him cheating shortly after I told him. God is so good.

Remember you all it takes a real man or woman to accept the fact that I could have had sex with someone else, but I love God too much to disappoint Him. Glory to God. I just got happy!

You may ask, "Why did she tell him anything since she didn't have any sexual contact, no kiss, nothing of that sort?"

If I could not share this with my better half, my friend, my husband and my lover, then what? I wanted to have my feelings out on the front line. No secrets! I wanted to share this with my spouse, not to make him jealous, but to let him know I needed him to pray for me.

Don't Let "*The Tail*" Bring You Down

CHAPTER 12

Final Warning

Delilah brought Samson down. Bathsheba brought David down. Solomon was brought down by the love of women. John was killed for speaking out against sexual sins. He preached, "Repent for the kingdom of heaven is at hand." He preached against adultery, and he was killed for telling the king about his relationship with his brother's wife.

I know this book will be criticized for speaking against sexually immoral sins, but I will stand for righteousness. I don't care who calls me "holy roller" and sets out to take my life.

I will forever say, "Repent. Turn from your wicked ways. God wants to save you."

You may be a housewife, billionaire, blue-collar worker, or even the president. God wants to change your life today. He wants to give you a new relationship in Him.

Please understand you are being brought down by the lust of women or men. This is the last hour. The call has been made. Never in my life have I seen so many preachers, teachers, evangelists, deacons, singers, prophetesses, and workers in the church, being brought down because of the tail. Some are active in the church and are saying, "God has not left me." You're right.

Hebrews 13: says God will never leave nor will he forsake you, but you can forsake God. If you are reading this book, I know you are saying that God will forgive me. You are right. He will forgive, but we can't stay in our sins. "Present your body a living sacrifice, holy, and acceptable unto God as your reasonable service." (Roman 12:1-2)

I know this book will probably not be popular among some of my brothers and sisters in Christ, but I plead with you today. Repent for the Kingdom of Heaven is at hand. God is getting ready to expose all the evil works that are behind closed doors. Choose Him today. God is waiting on you.

You are on your way to a burning hell, if you don't repent from your sins. You are blind and cannot see how the devil is laughing at you. Come out of her. Revelation 18:4 says "COME OUT OF HER." Today, I pray you make a choice right now.

If you knew the amount of people I have talked to concerning lust and sexual sins, you would be surprised how many are caught up in sexual sin.

This is not just for young people, but I'm talking to the elderly as well.

Just the other day, I was talking with a lady who is in her late 60's, and she's single. She is still struggling with the sexual demon. Oh, it never stops.

This book is a sign and a warning to every believer and nonbeliever. There will be a day when sex will not rule.

God is getting ready to bring his wrath on the church if the church does not turn back to Him.

No longer will those who are indulged in sexual immorality be allowed to direct the choir or even play instruments. No longer will the spirit of Eli's sons be allow to stand at the door of the choir seeking to lay with the women and men of the church. Leaders will soon be brought down for taking advantage of God's people. God is getting ready to bring judgment to the house of God. Come out of her so that you will not share in her sins. Today you can change.

Pray for yourself and your leader. This harlot has been exposed. You have the knowledge about her and the dragon's tail. I pray you get out today in Jesus Name.

God sees you. He is watching, and He cares. Hell is hot. It will not be long. Jesus will return. My brothers and sisters, I pray that you keep your lamps trimmed and burning.

LISTEN, STOP SINNING and LIVE.

Acknowledgments

I would like to thank God and my family for allowing me to release this book with no apology. Everything you read in this book is true and very true. Thank you Roderick Mitchell for allowing me to share with God's people without being a shame of our past. Thank you Tyna Porter for designing and formatting this book. Also Lisa Bell thanks so much for editing the book. Min. Marcus Synder for photo in red and Annie for outside photo. I would like to thank Pastor Ed Synder for forwarding this book. God bless all of you for always supporting me.

About The Author

If this book has been a blessing to you, please tell someone about it. We must spread the message and expose the devil and this Harlot.

I would like to thank God for all those who prayed for me on this journey. God has shared so many prophetic things concerning sexual sins. He has revealed the Harlot and the beast like never before.

Jesus is soon to come. Will you let sexual sins prevent you from entering into the Kingdom of Heaven? Will you follow after pleasure and burn in the Lake of Fire forever? I pray you examine yourself and ask God to forgive you. God loves you. Please show him, you love him too. LET YOUR LIGHT SHINE! Come out of the Harlot!

Contact Information
Barbara Mitchell
Barbaramitchellministries@gmail.com
www.BarbaraMitchellministry.com
P.O Box 170294
Irving, TX 75017
972-310-0386

I have known Pastor Barbara Mitchell for a short while, but in this window of time I am impressed with her love, not only for God, but His Kingdom. To say she has been through a lot…is an understatement. So, the following pages are written under a very special anointing brought out of the fire of adversity and pain.

Pastor Mitchell has written about a subject that has been labeled 'taboo' in the church. It is a subject that no one wants to talk about in fear we might offend. It is a subject that has not been addressed and then we wonder why it is so prevalent in the church. Yes, that is the subject of sex. There I said it, and now Pastor Mitchell will take you on a journey, not only exposing the source of this sin that has plagued the church for years, but bring it out in the open and deal with its very nature.

Get ready to feel uncomfortable as you read these pages of written ministry. This empowers you in "how to deal with this sin" so you can finally be free of this secret sin that has brought down the best of the best. There are some who we thought would never succumb to it's slithering deception and even to justify it in their heart and mind that it is somehow acceptable.

Don't let the tail bring you down. Read this book, study its content and apply it to your mind and spirit. Let us finally be free of this secret sin and talk about it.

God bless you as you become at liberty in God's unwavering power against sin.

Pastor Ed Synder

www.ingramcontent.com/pod-product-compliance
Lightning Source LLC
Chambersburg PA
CBHW020807160426
43192CB00006B/474